Adult Color by Numbers Coloring Book

Enjoy coloring stunning nature scenes

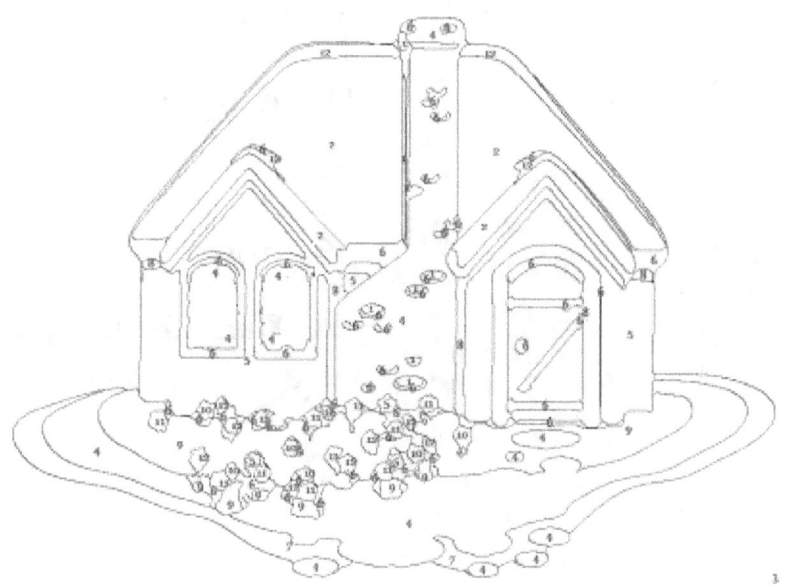

Copyright © 2020 Adult Puzzle Books

1. Black
2. Blue
3. Green
4. Red
5. Dark Red
6. Orange
7. Yellow
8. Purple
9. Gold
10. Pink
11. Light Blue
12. Grey
13. Brown
14. Dark Green

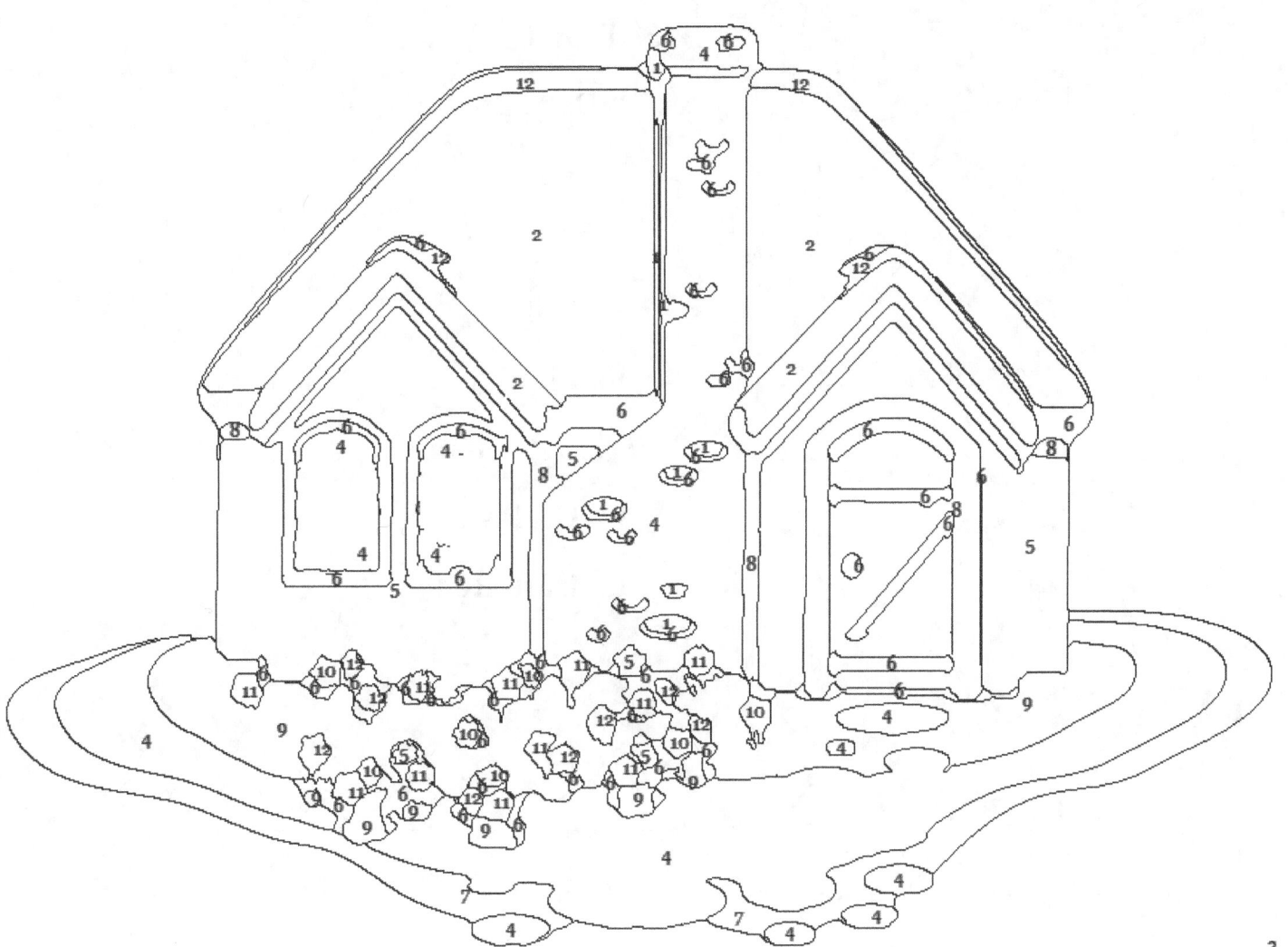

1. Black
2. Yellow
3. Grey
4. Blue
5. Brown
6. Dark Brown
7. Red
8. Purple
9. Gold
10. Pink
11. Light Blue
12. Dark Green
13. Dark Red

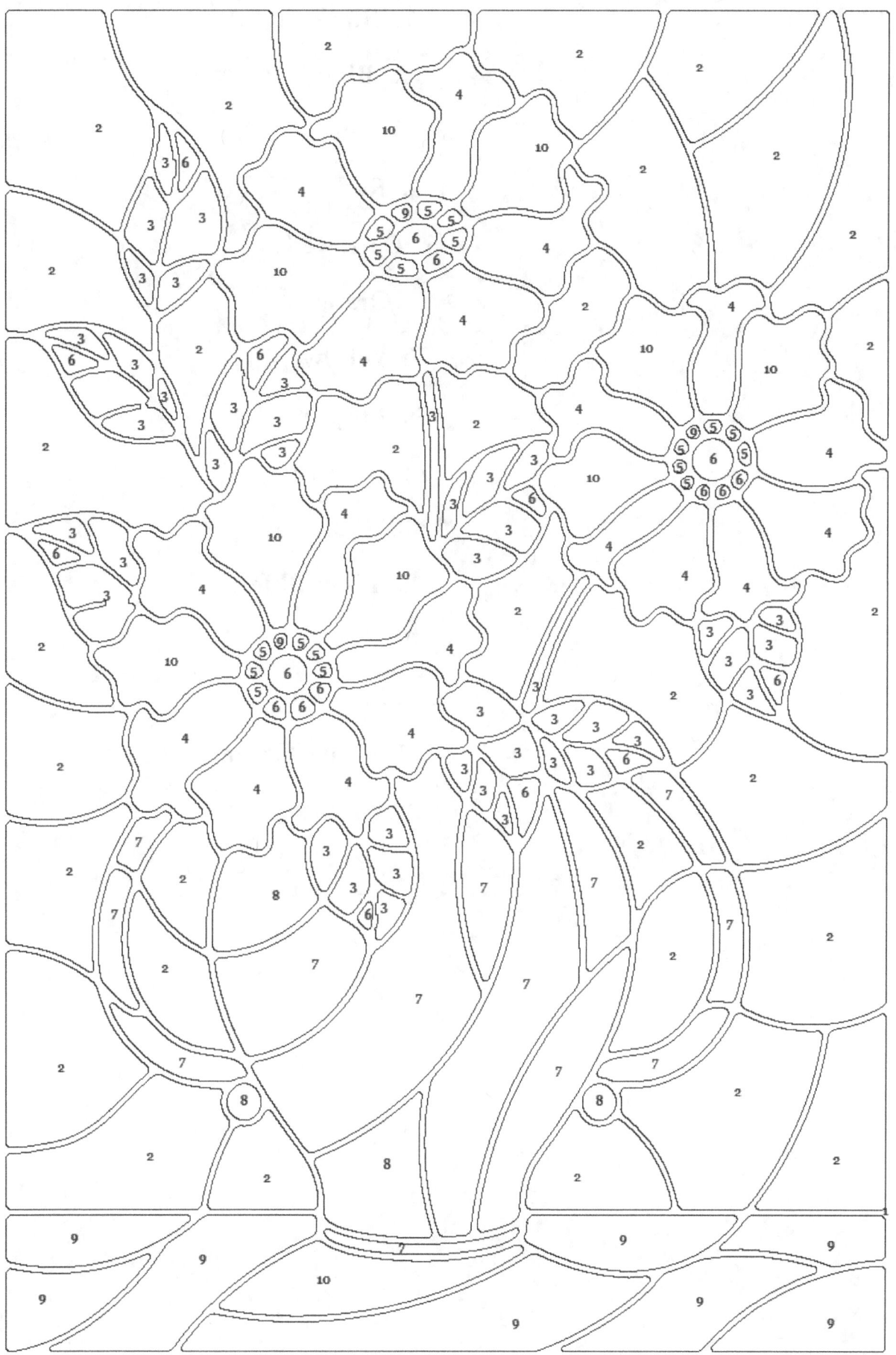

1. Black
2. Blue
3. Green
4. Red
5. Dark Red
6. Orange
7. Yellow
8. Purple
9. Gold
10. Pink
11. Light Blue
12. Grey
13. Brown
14. Dark Green

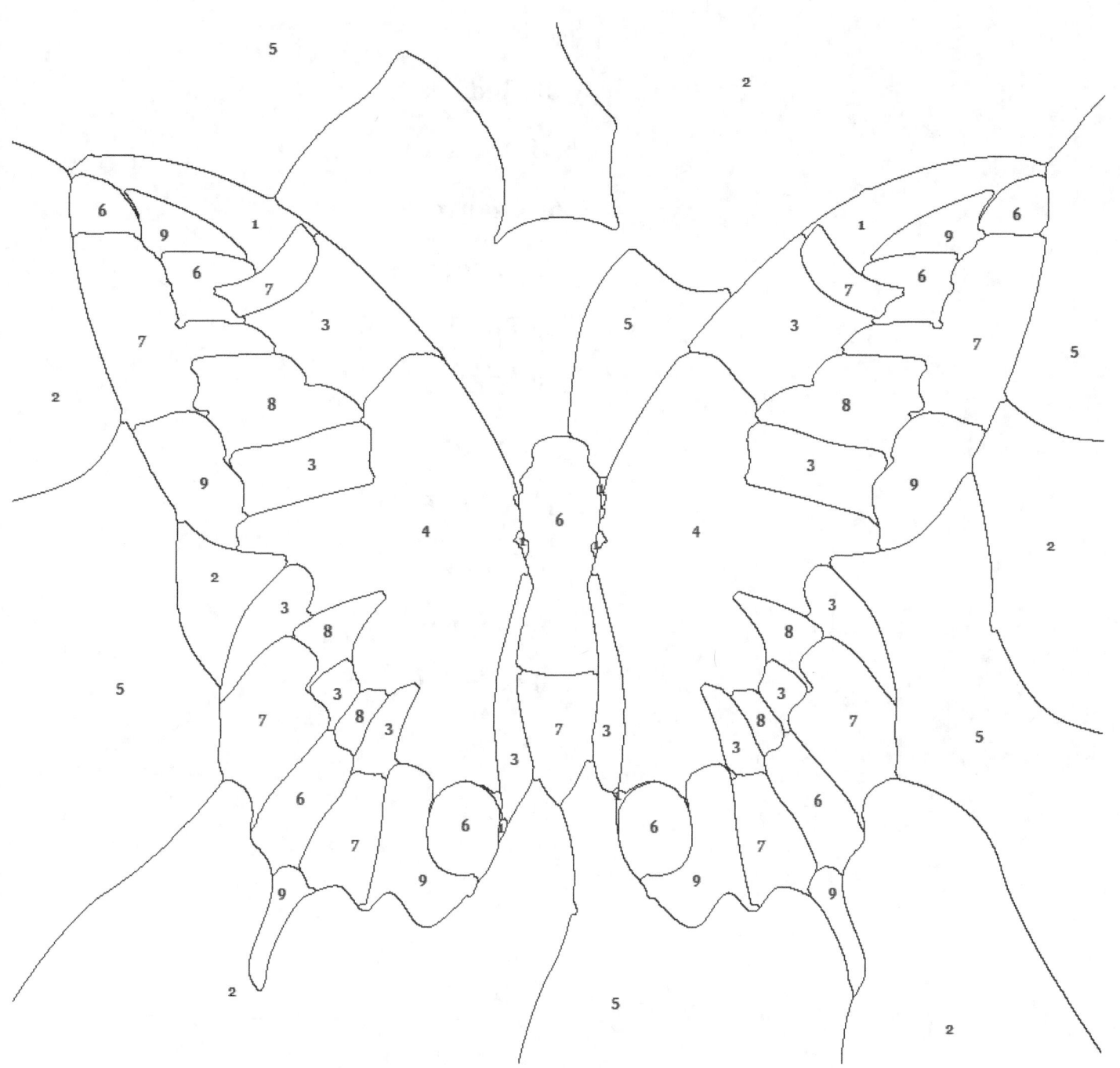

1. Black
2. Blue
3. Green
4. Red
5. Dark Red
6. Orange
7. Yellow
8. Purple
9. Gold
10. Pink
11. Light Blue
12. Grey
13. Brown
14. Dark Green

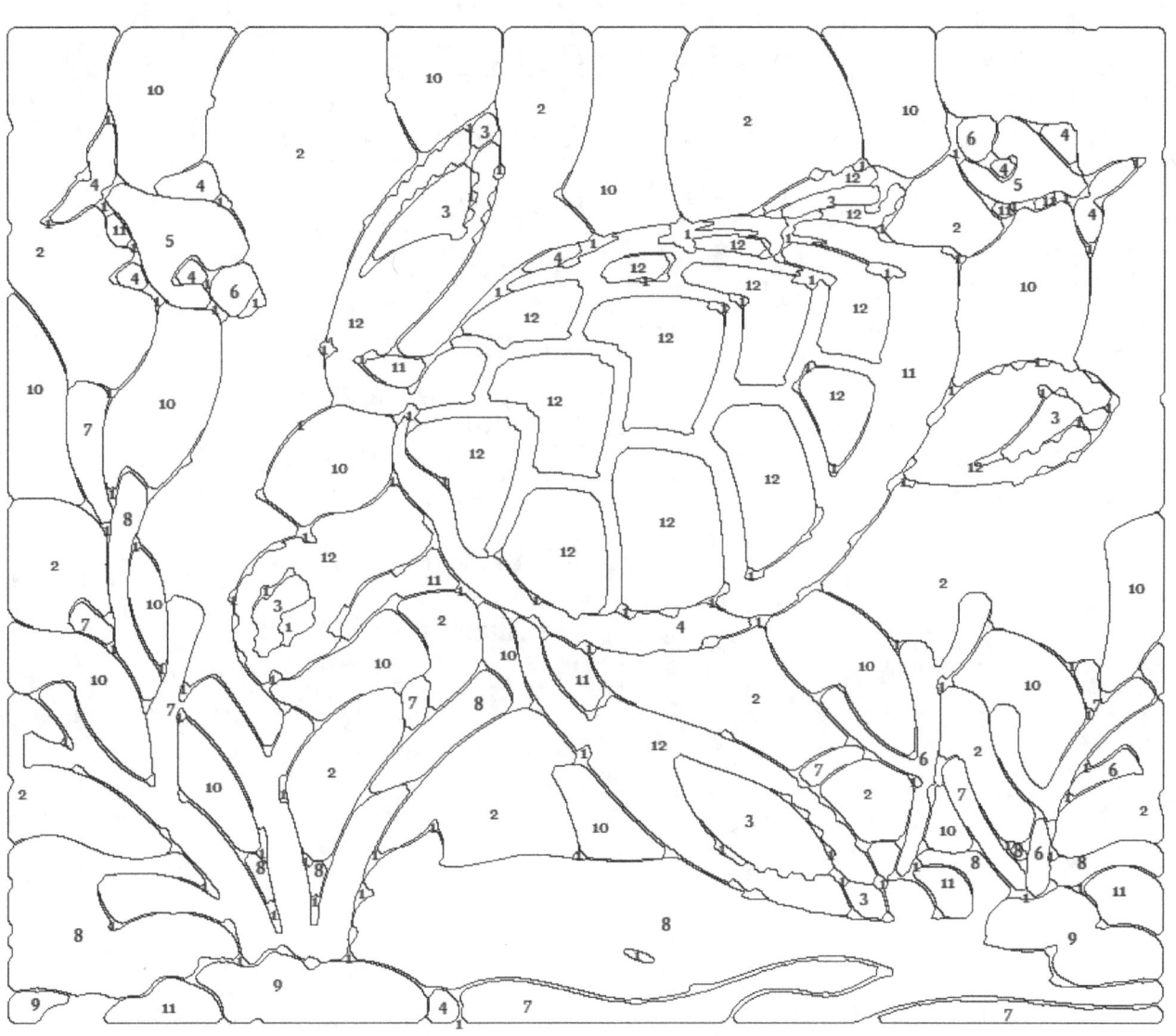

1. Black
2. Blue
3. Green
4. Red
5. Dark Red
6. Orange
7. Yellow
8. Purple
9. Gold
10. Pink
11. Light Blue
12. Grey
13. Brown
14. Dark Green

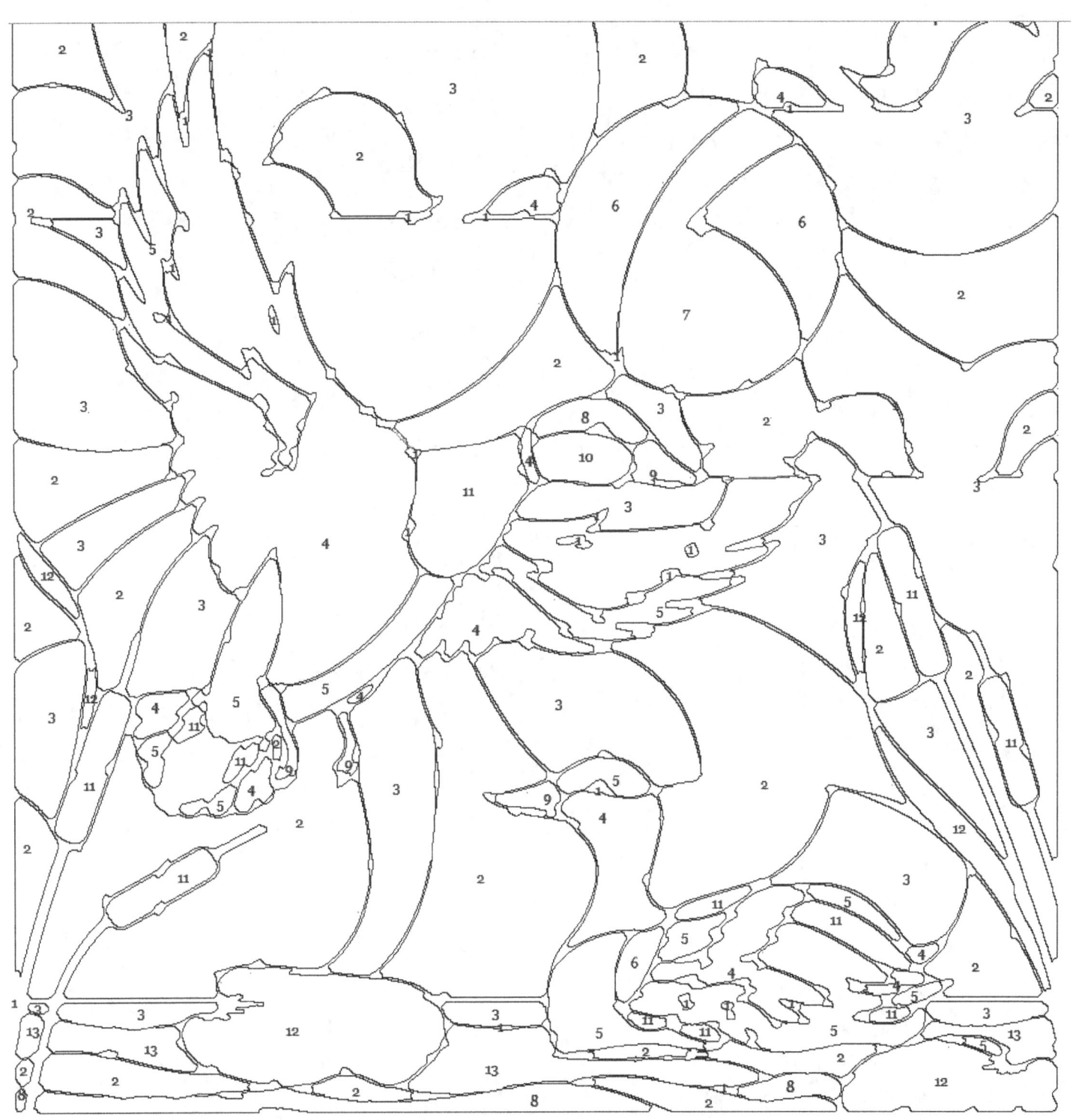

1. Black
2. Blue
3. Green
4. Red
5. Dark Red
6. Orange
7. Yellow
8. Purple
9. Gold
10. Pink
11. Light Blue
12. Grey
13. Brown
14. Dark Green

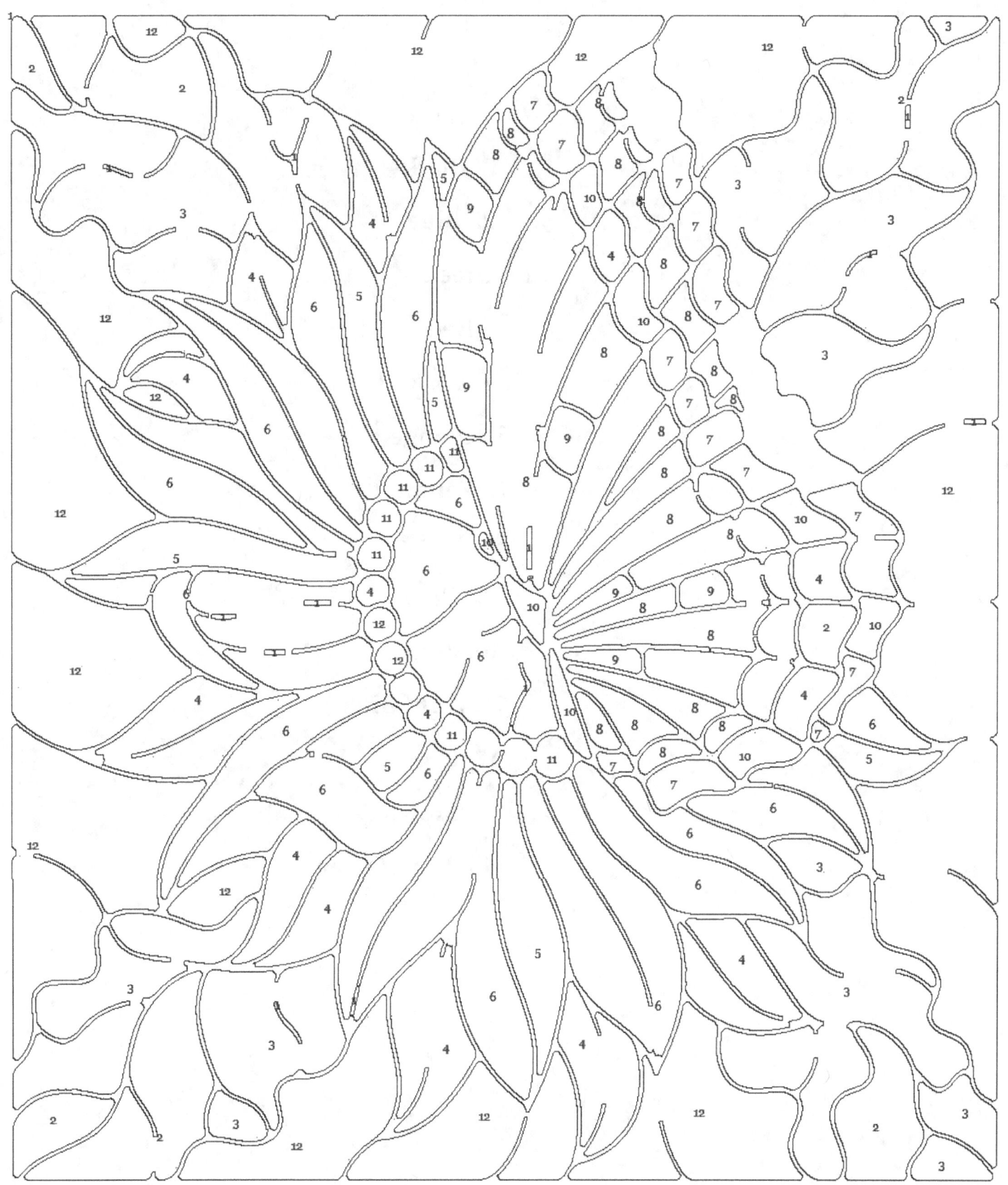

1. Black
2. Blue
3. Green
4. Red
5. Dark Red
6. Orange
7. Yellow
8. Purple
9. Gold
10. Pink
11. Light Blue
12. Grey
13. Brown
14. Dark Green

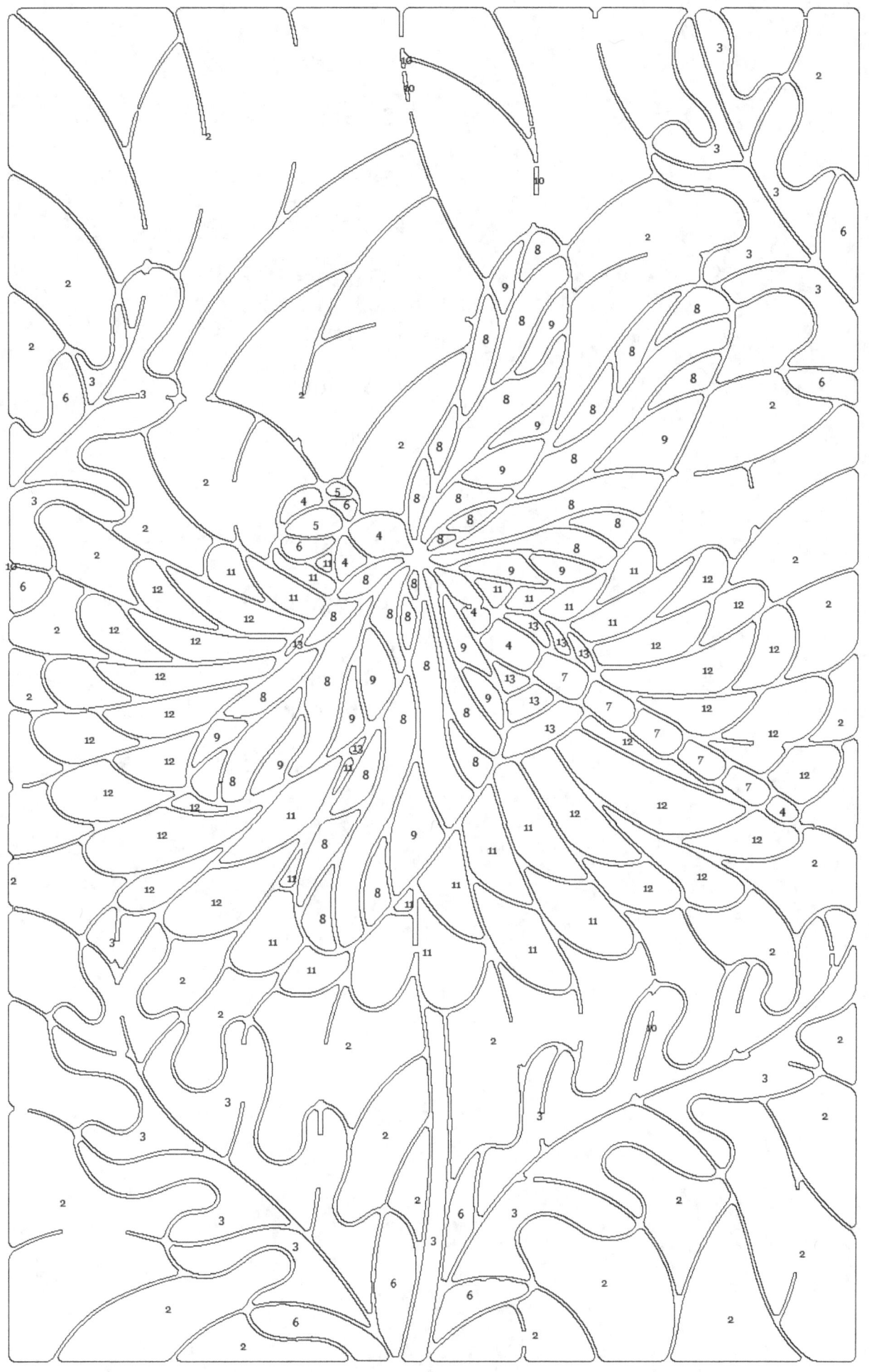

1. Black
2. Blue
3. Green
4. Red
5. Dark Red
6. Orange
7. Yellow
8. Purple
9. Gold
10. Pink
11. Light Blue
12. Grey
13. Brown
14. Dark Green

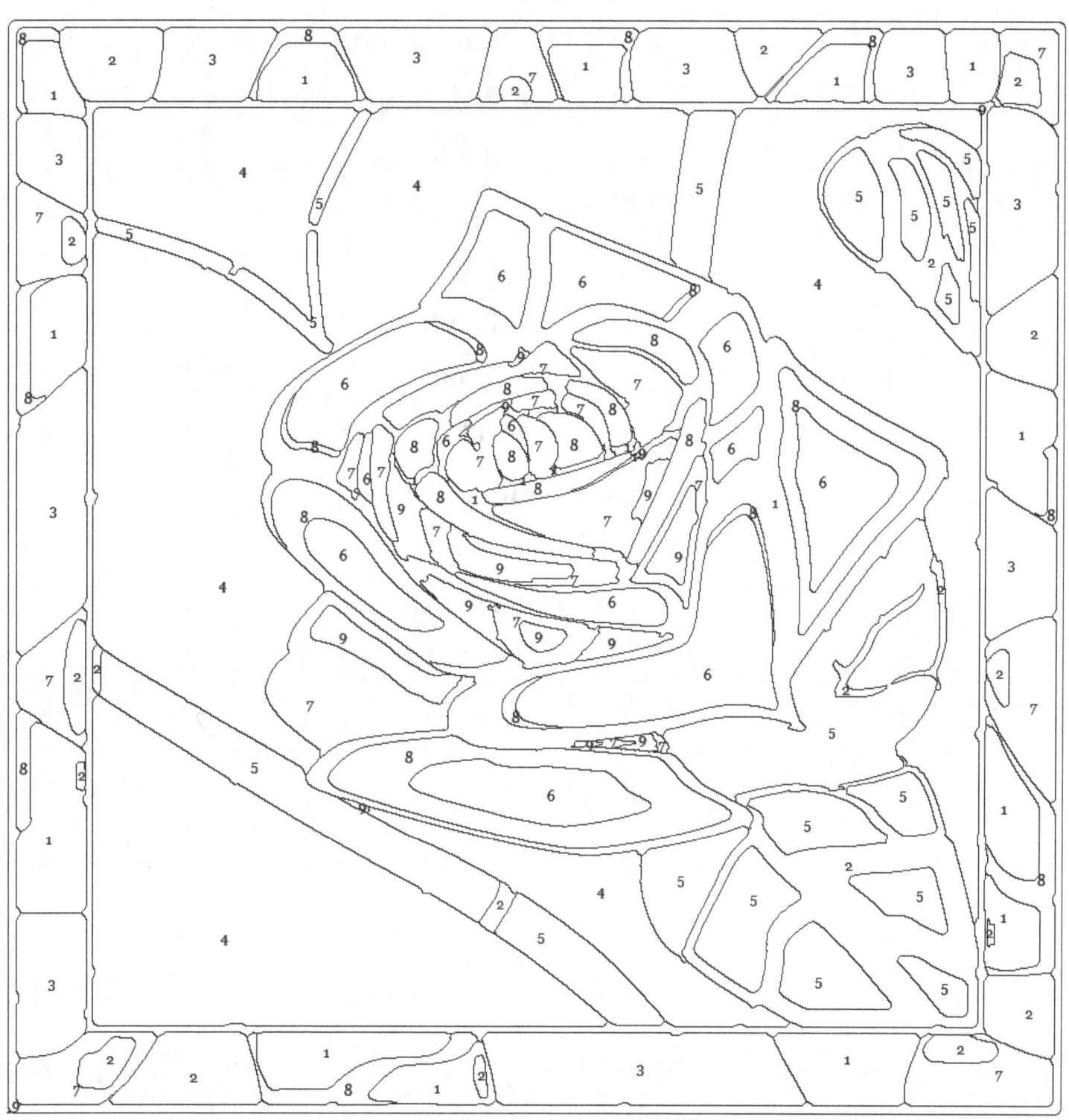

1. Black
2. Blue
3. Green
4. Red
5. Dark Red
6. Orange
7. Yellow
8. Purple
9. Gold
10. Pink
11. Light Blue
12. Grey
13. Brown
14. Dark Green

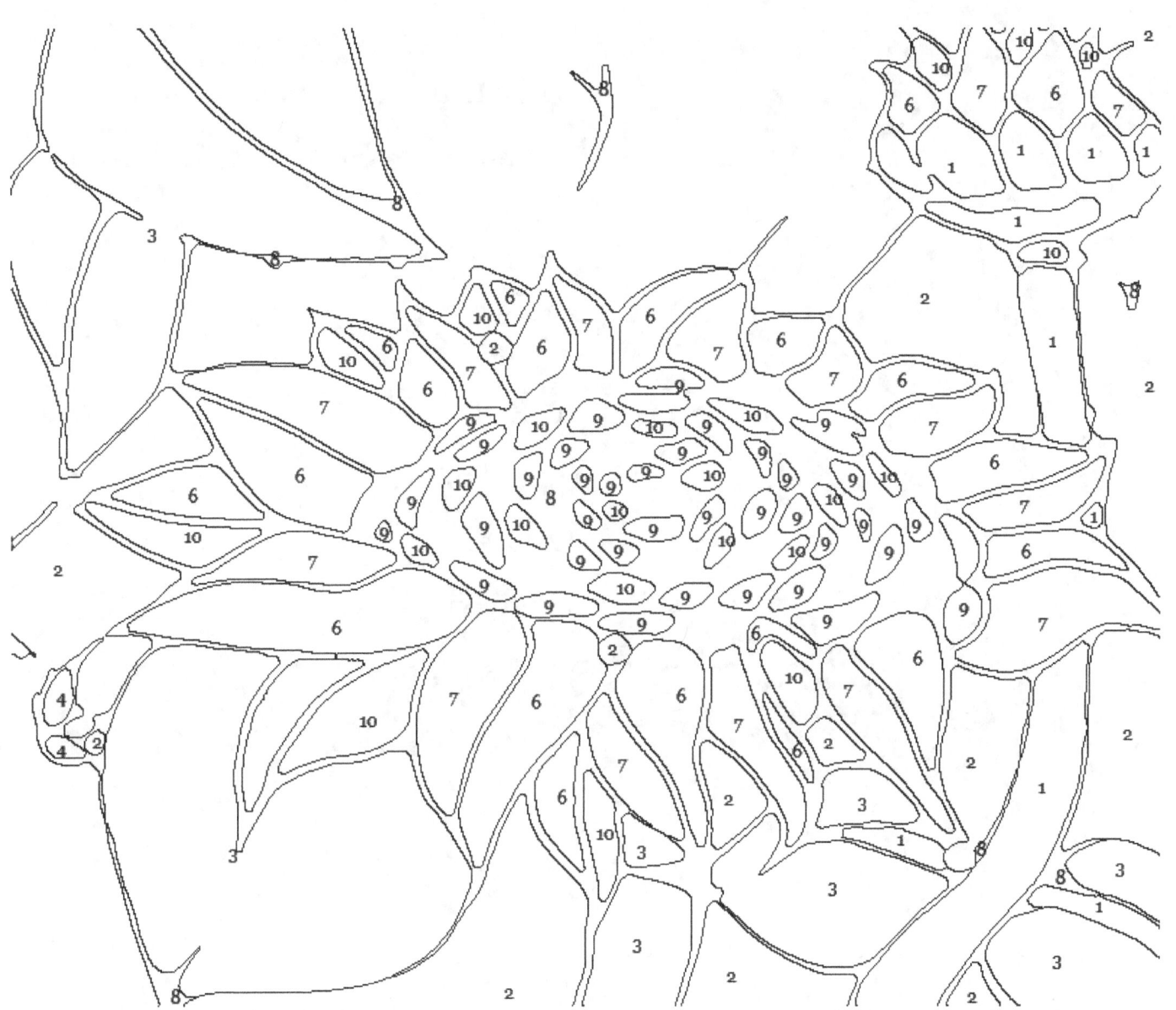

1. Black
2. Blue
3. Green
4. Red
5. Dark Red
6. Orange
7. Yellow
8. Purple
9. Gold
10. Pink
11. Light Blue
12. Grey
13. Brown
14. Dark Green

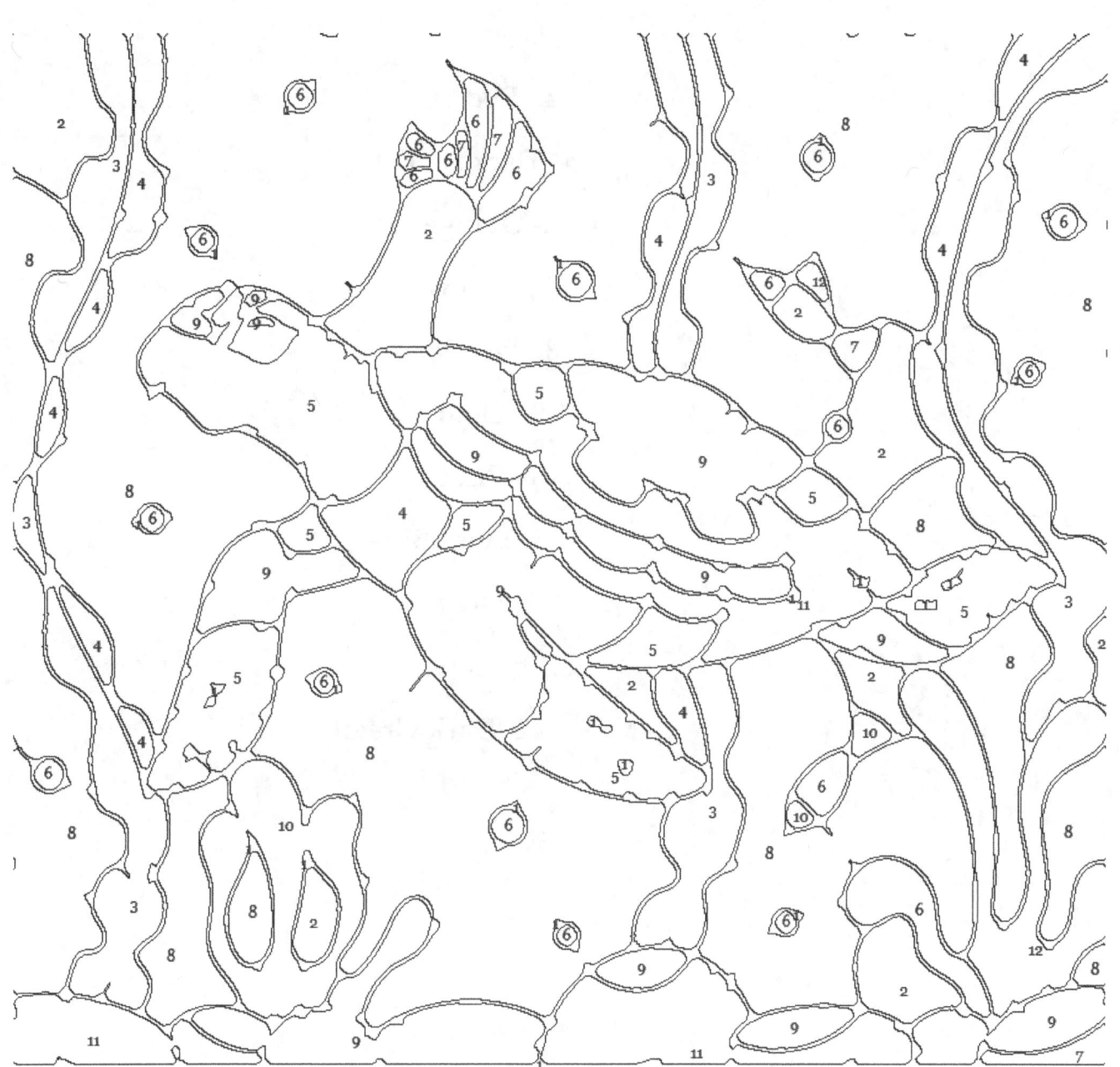

1. Black
2. Blue
3. Green
4. Red
5. Dark Red
6. Orange
7. Yellow
8. Purple
9. Gold
10. Pink
11. Light Blue
12. Grey
13. Brown
14. Dark Green

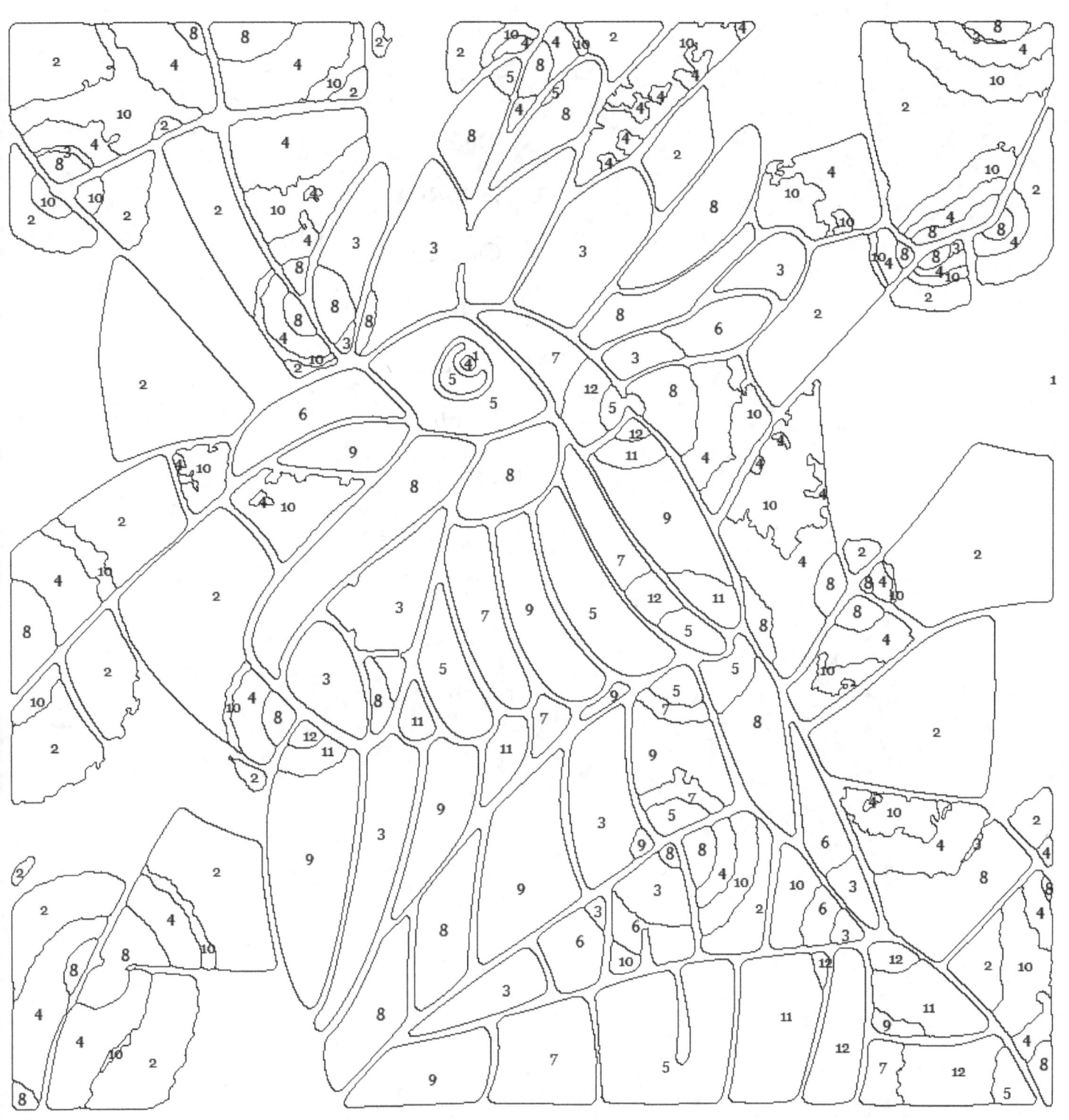

1. Black
2. Blue
3. Green
4. Red
5. Dark Red
6. Orange
7. Yellow
8. Purple
9. Gold
10. Pink
11. Light Blue
12. Grey
13. Brown
14. Dark Green

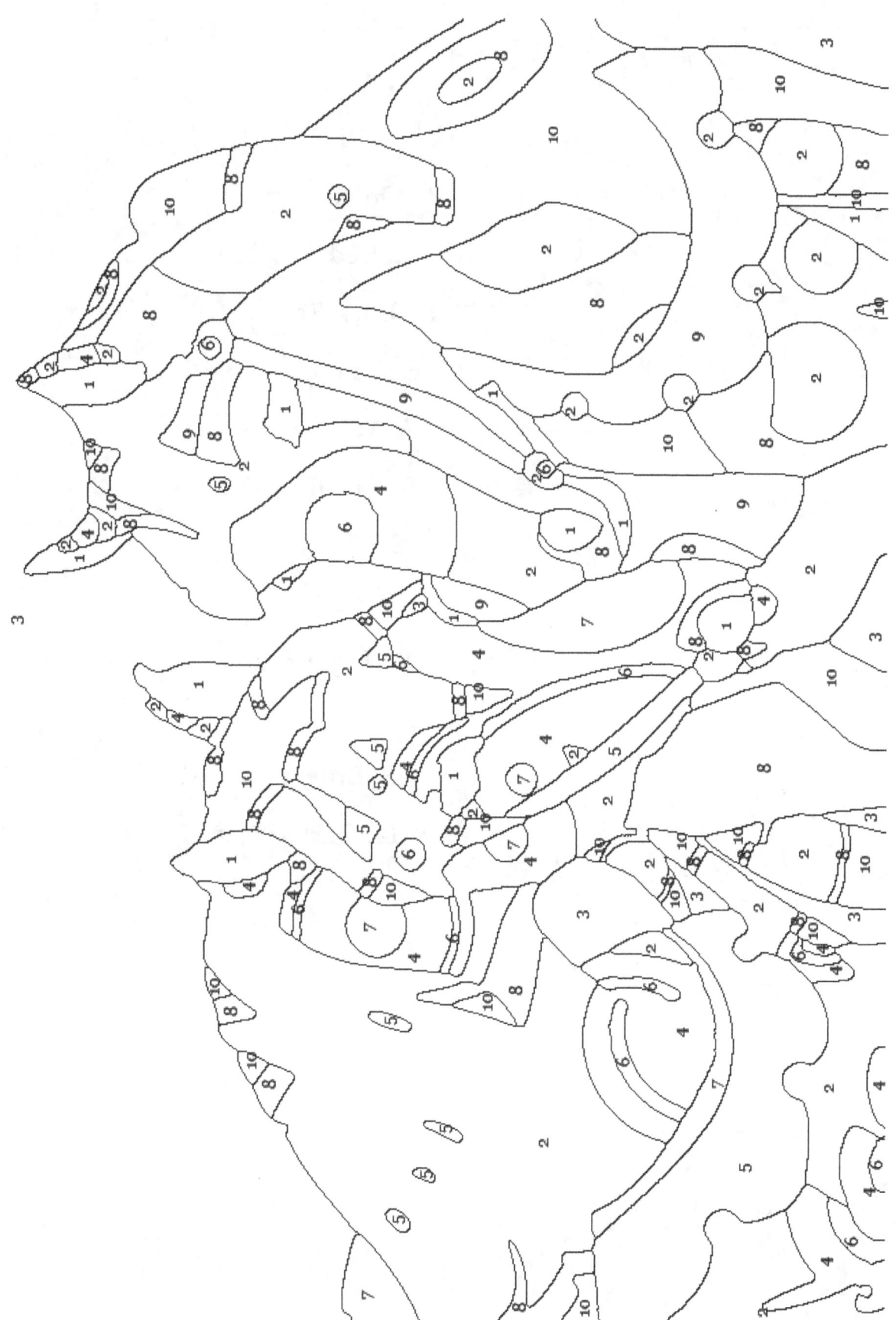

1. Black
2. Blue
3. Green
4. Red
5. Dark Red
6. Orange
7. Yellow
8. Purple
9. Gold
10. Pink
11. Light Blue
12. Grey
13. Brown
14. Dark Green

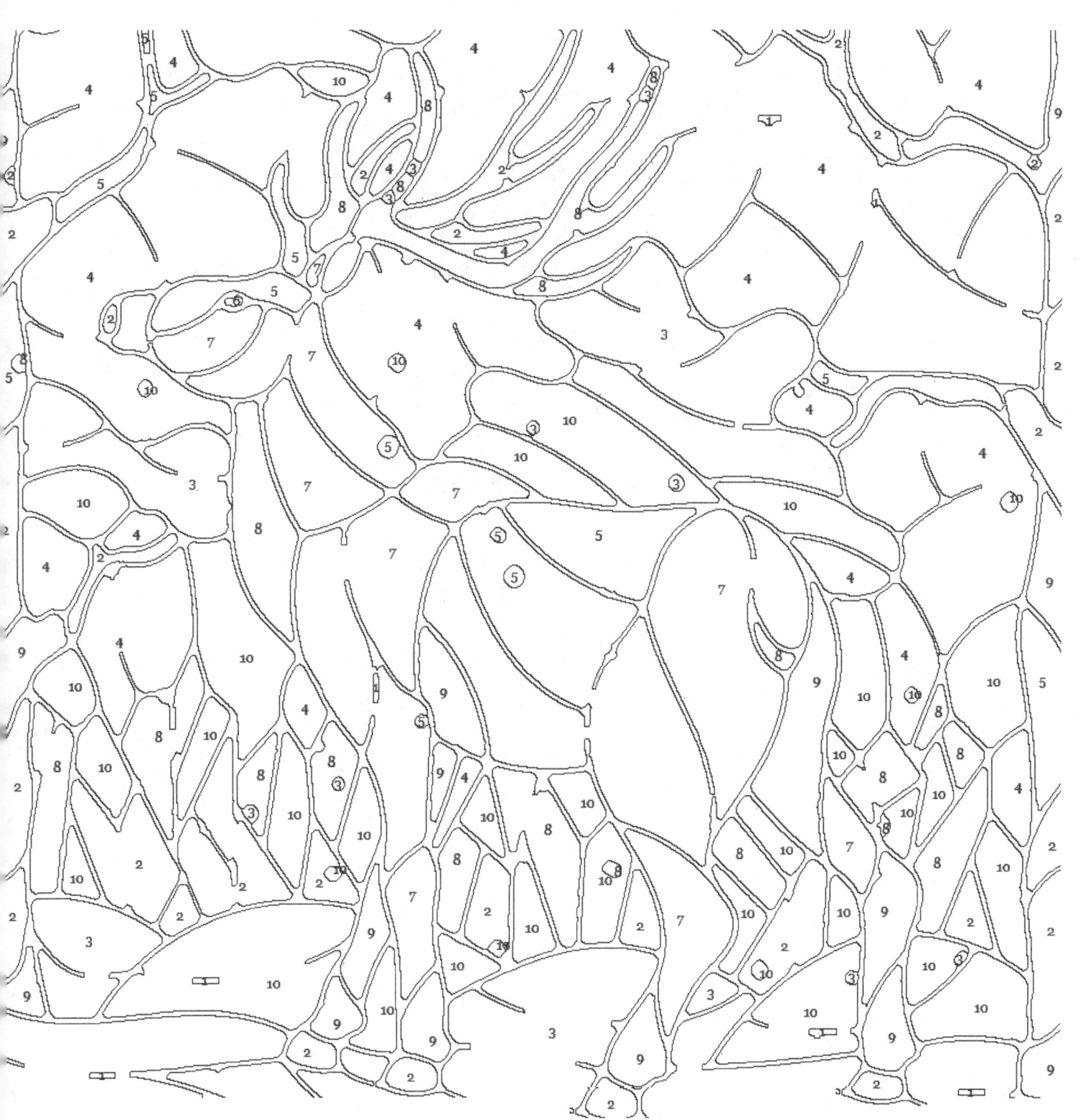

1. Black
2. Blue
3. Green
4. Red
5. Dark Red
6. Orange
7. Yellow
8. Purple
9. Gold
10. Pink
11. Light Blue
12. Grey
13. Brown
14. Dark Green

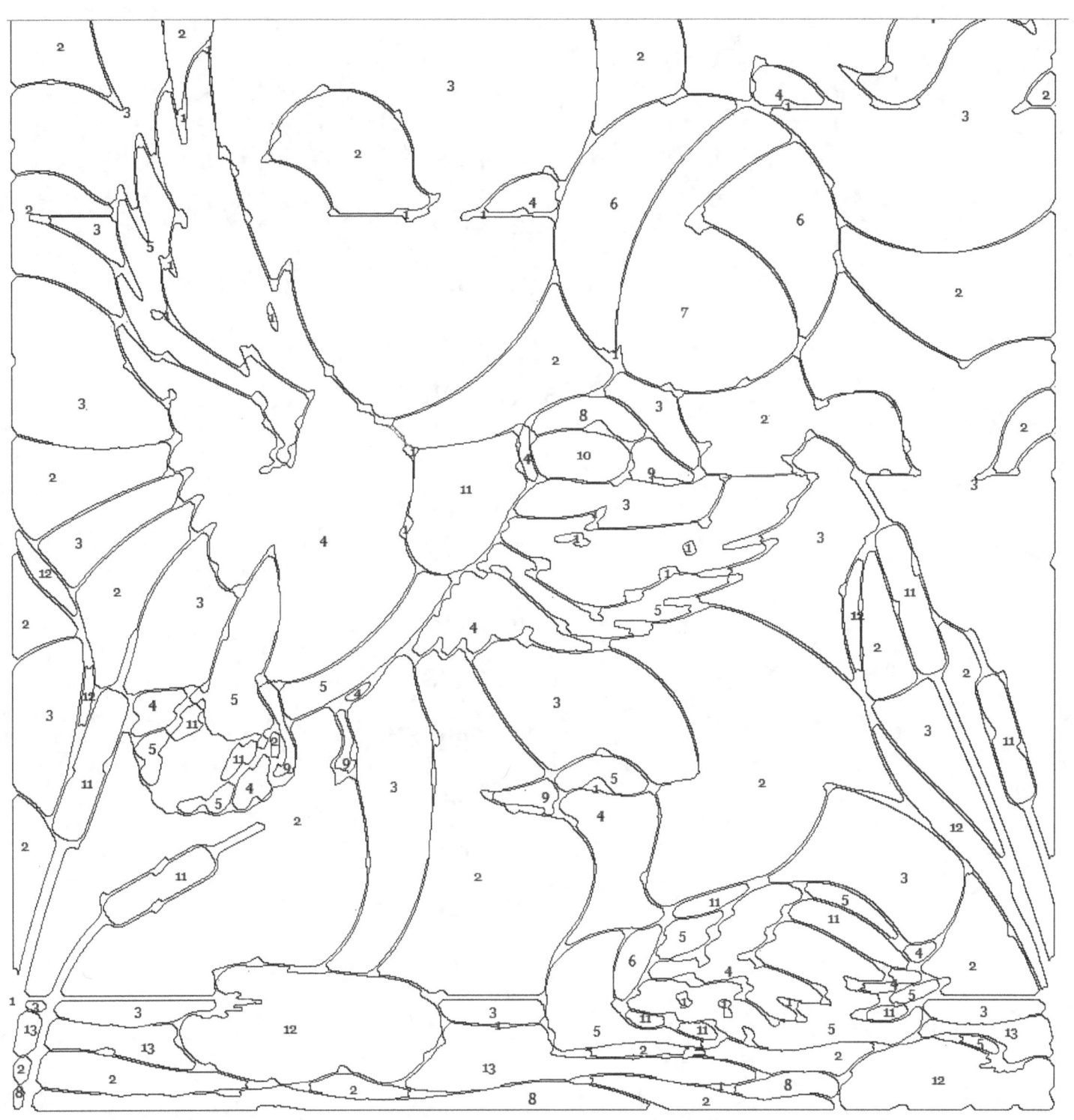

1. Black
2. Blue
3. Green
4. Red
5. Dark Red
6. Orange
7. Yellow
8. Purple
9. Gold
10. Pink
11. Light Blue
12. Grey
13. Brown
14. Dark Green

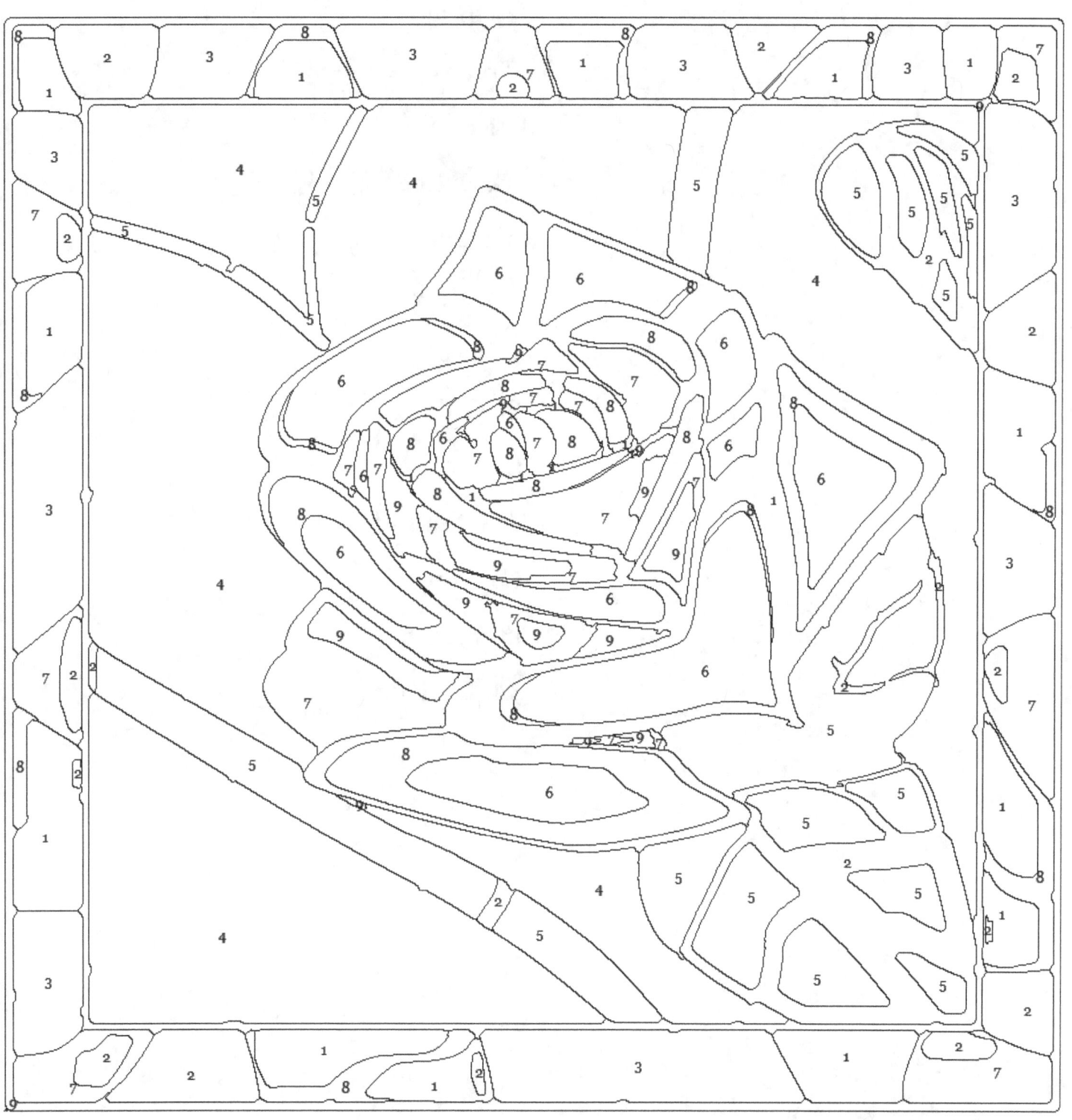

1. Black
2. Blue
3. Green
4. Red
5. Dark Red
6. Orange
7. Yellow
8. Purple
9. Gold
10. Pink
11. Light Blue
12. Grey
13. Brown
14. Dark Green

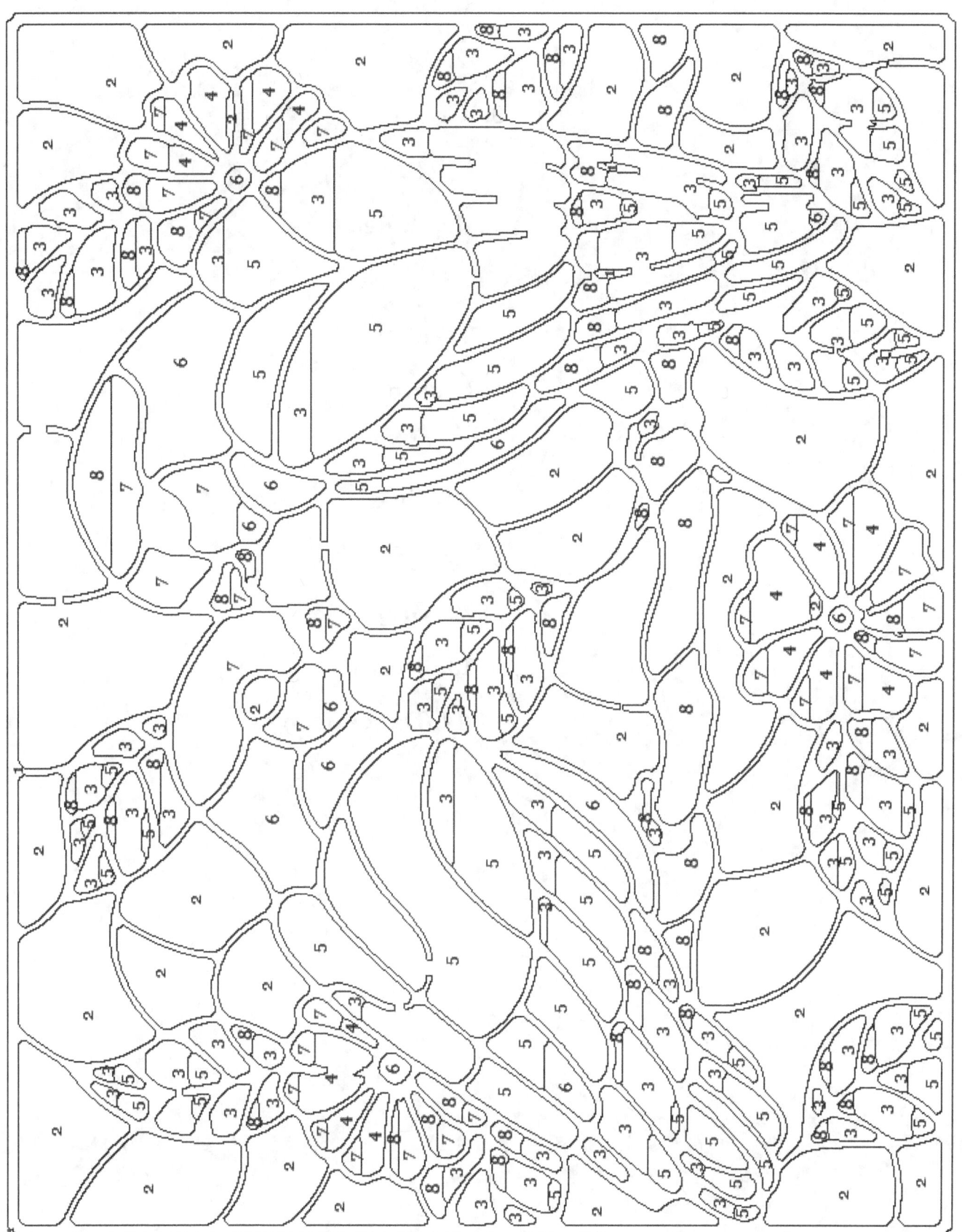

1. Black
2. Blue
3. Green
4. Red
5. Dark Red
6. Orange
7. Yellow
8. Purple
9. Gold
10. Pink
11. Light Blue
12. Grey
13. Brown
14. Dark Green

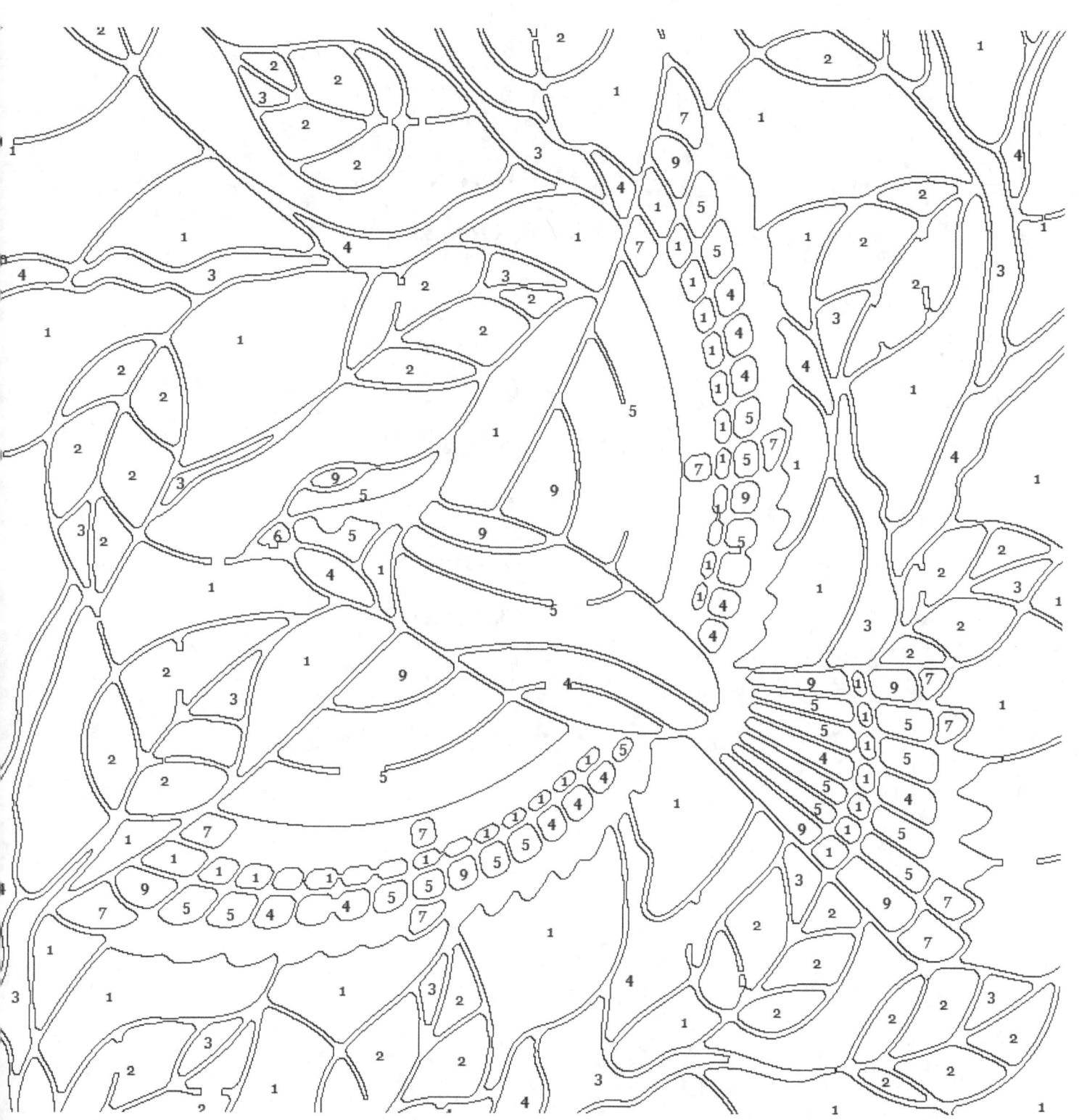

1. Black
2. Blue
3. Green
4. Red
5. Dark Red
6. Orange
7. Yellow
8. Purple
9. Gold
10. Pink
11. Light Blue
12. Grey
13. Brown
14. Dark Green

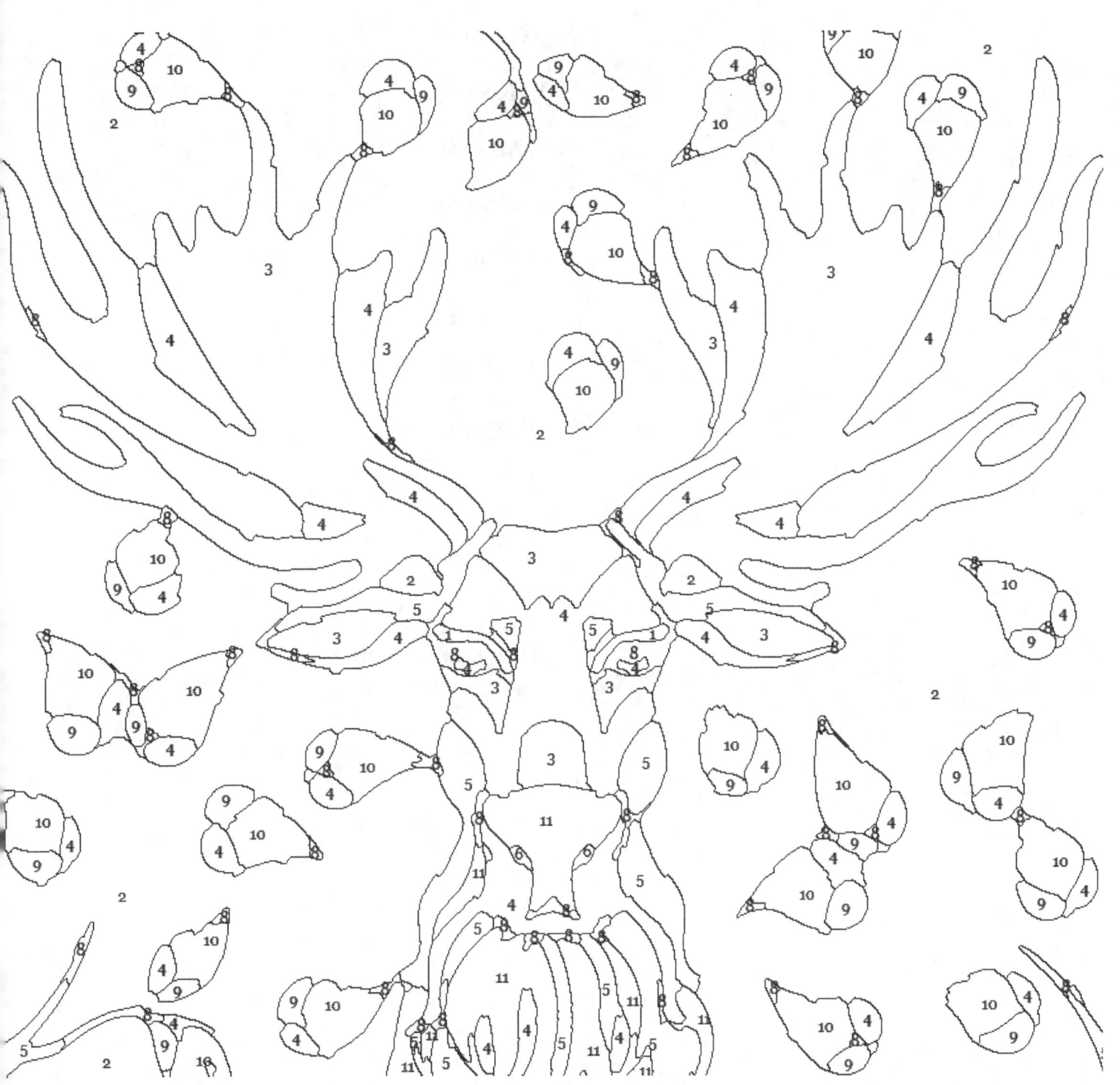

1. Black
2. Blue
3. Green
4. Red
5. Dark Red
6. Orange
7. Yellow
8. Purple
9. Gold
10. Pink
11. Light Blue
12. Grey
13. Brown
14. Dark Green

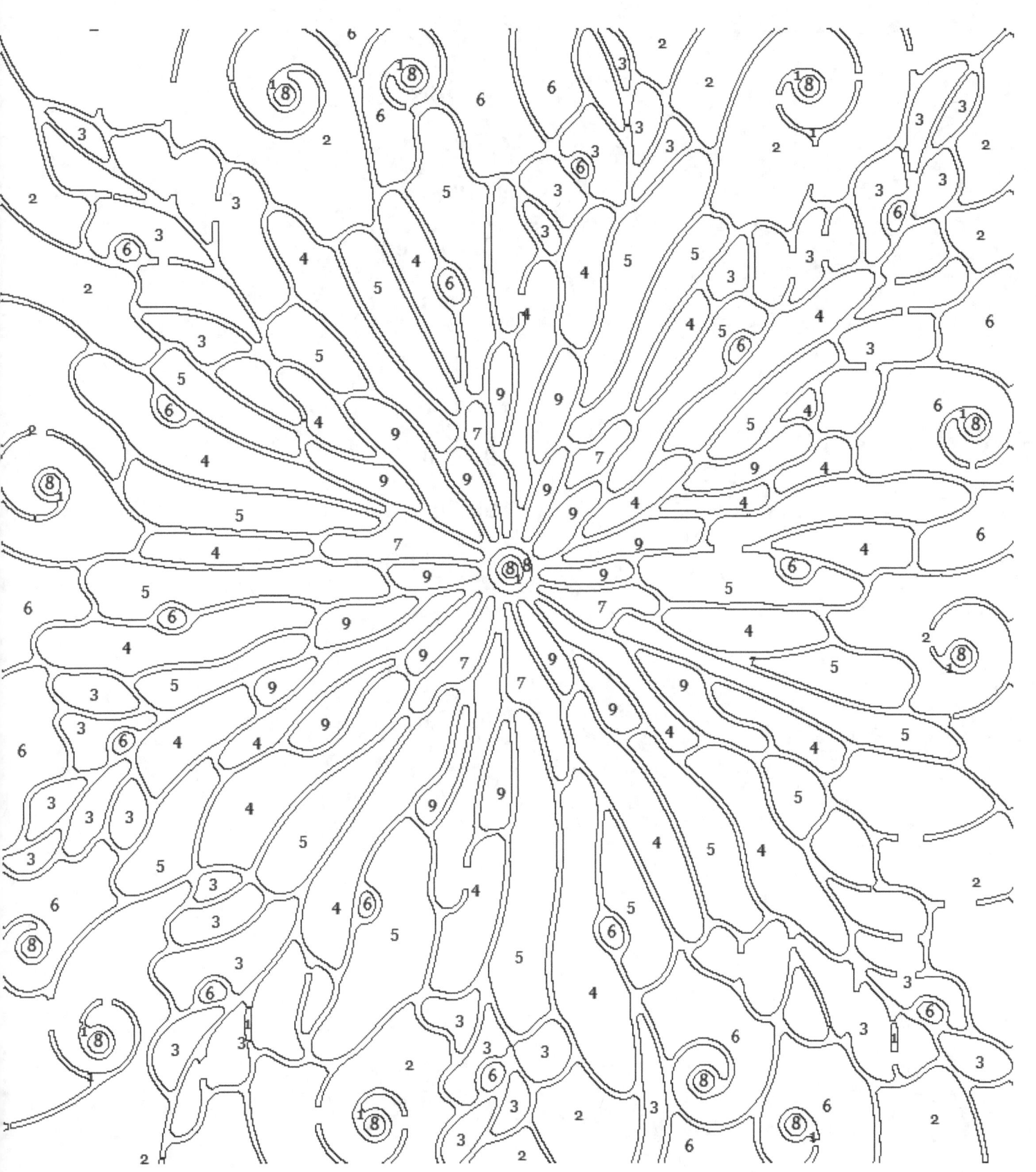

1. Black
2. Blue
3. Green
4. Red
5. Dark Red
6. Orange
7. Yellow
8. Purple
9. Gold
10. Pink
11. Light Blue
12. Grey
13. Brown
14. Dark Green

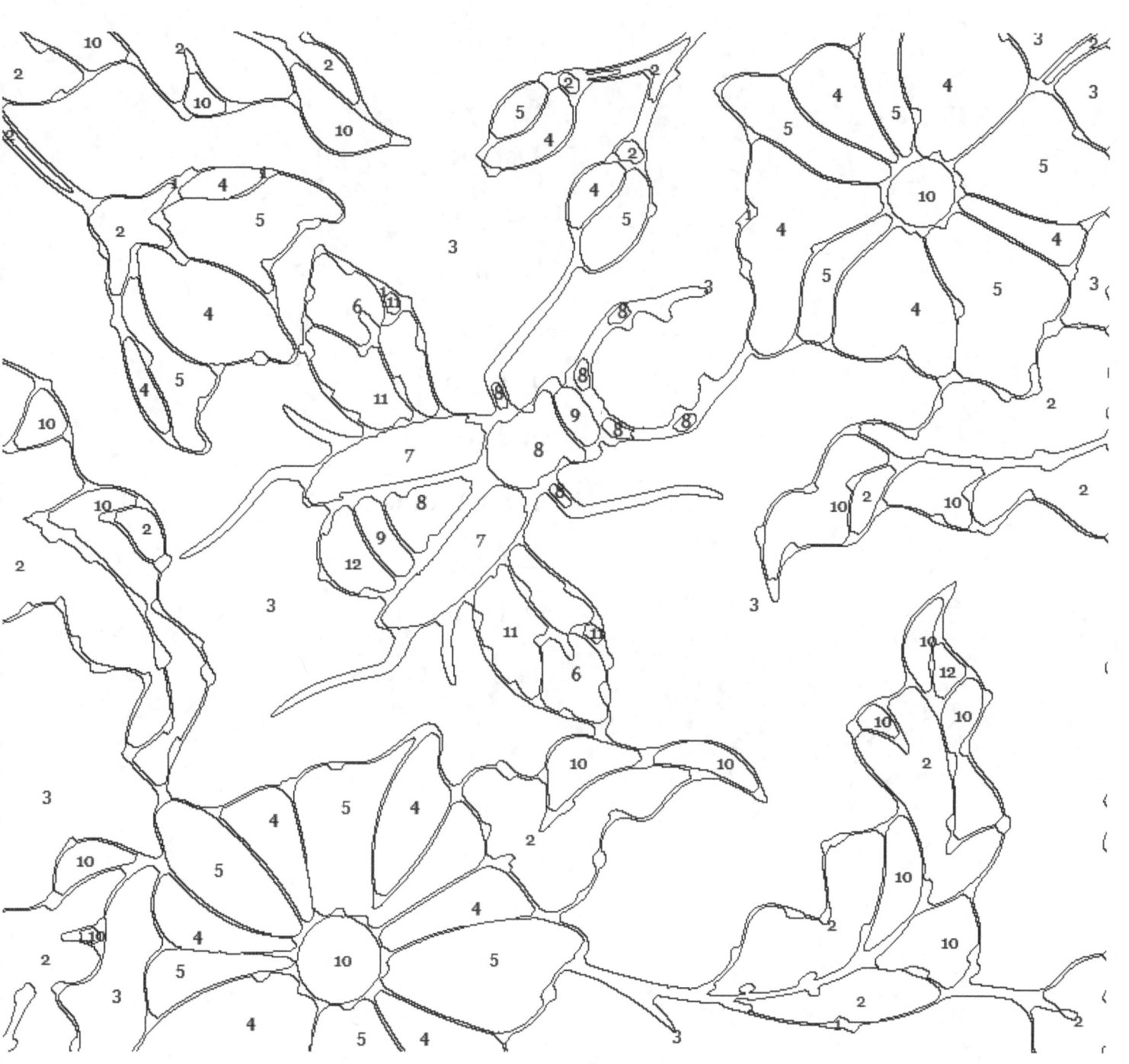

1. Black
2. Blue
3. Green
4. Red
5. Dark Red
6. Orange
7. Yellow
8. Purple
9. Gold
10. Pink
11. Light Blue
12. Grey
13. Brown
14. Dark Green

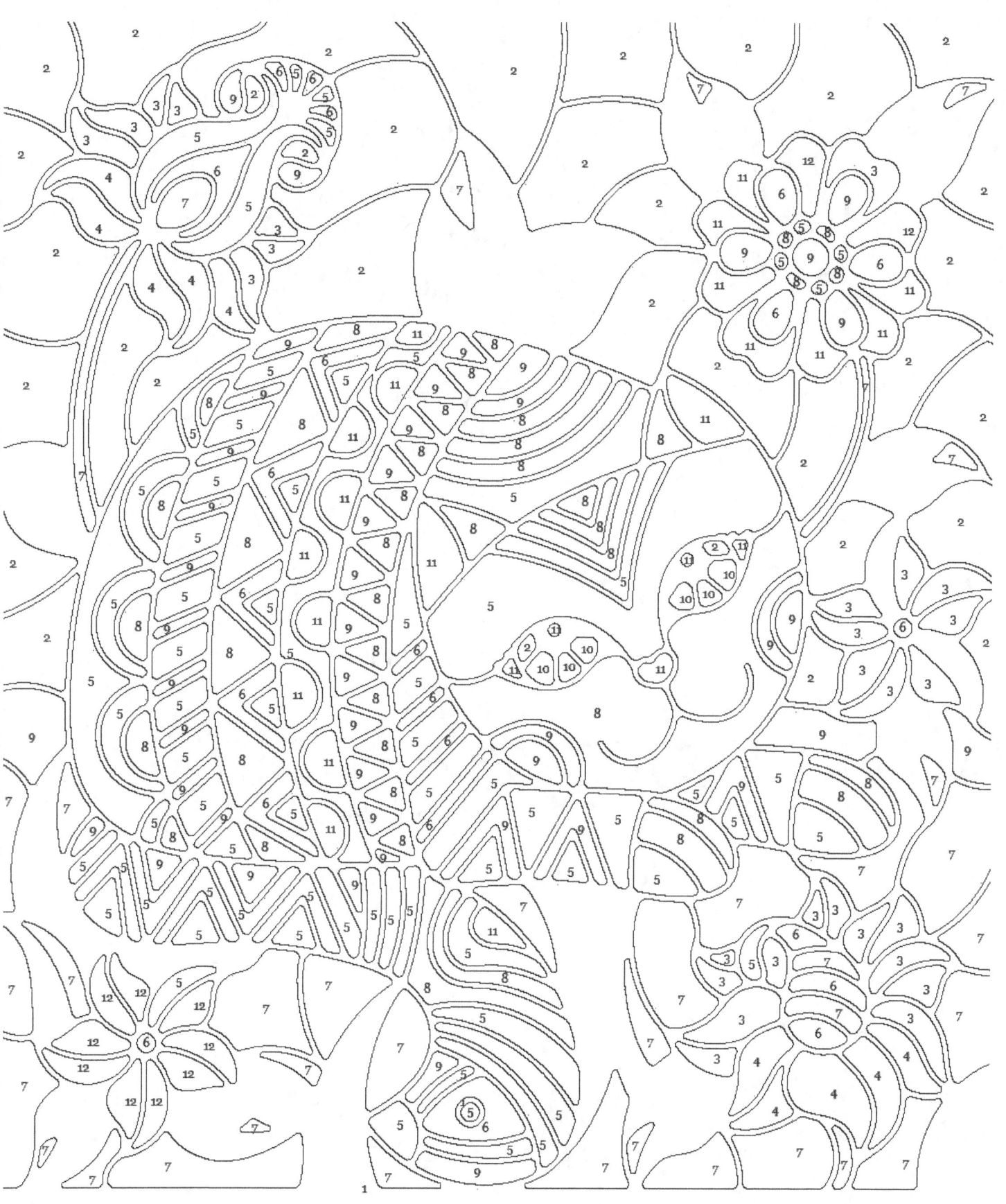

1. Black
2. Blue
3. Green
4. Red
5. Dark Red
6. Orange
7. Yellow
8. Purple
9. Gold
10. Pink
11. Light Blue
12. Grey
13. Brown
14. Dark Green

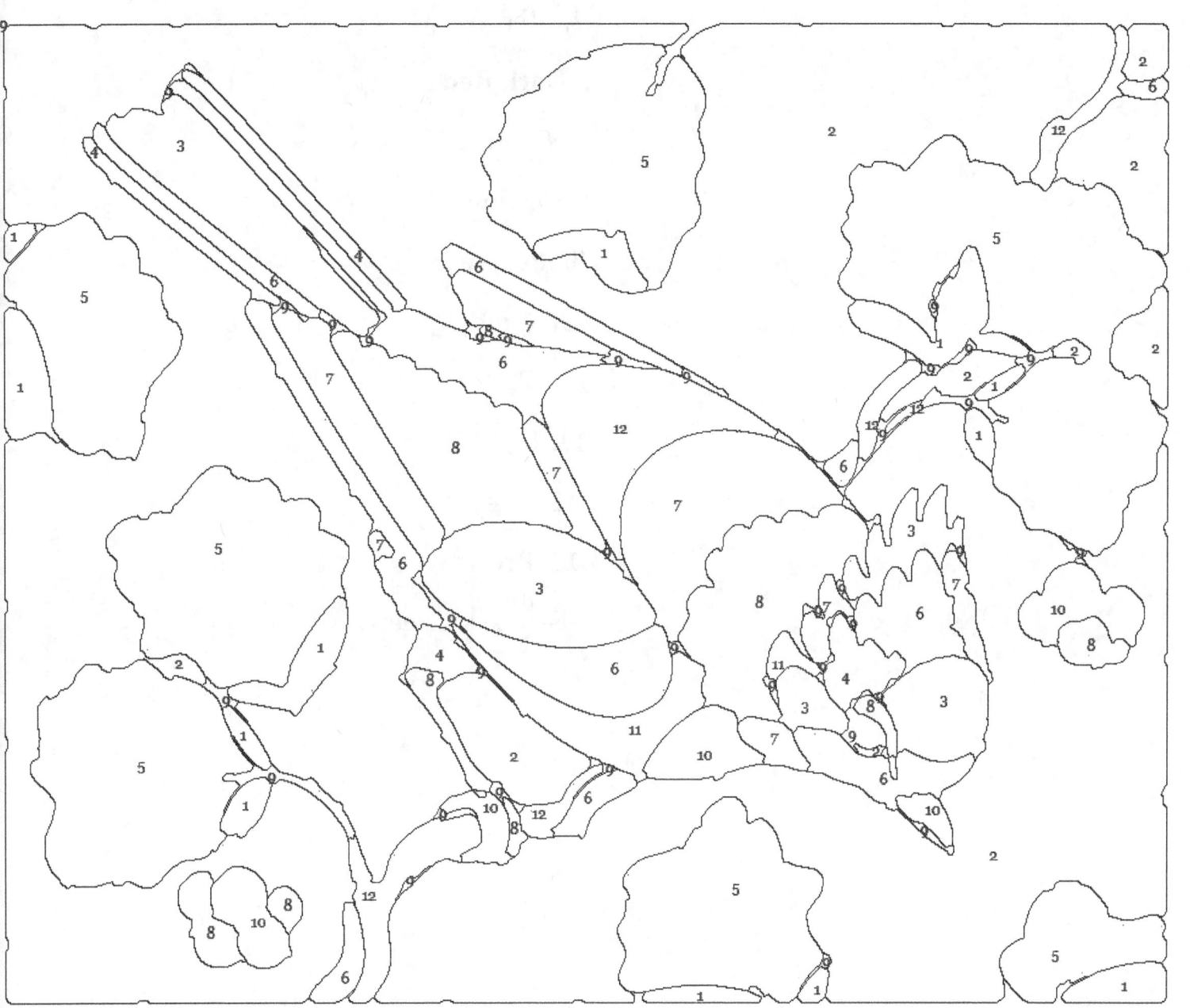

1. Black
2. Blue
3. Green
4. Red
5. Dark Red
6. Orange
7. Yellow
8. Purple
9. Gold
10. Pink
11. Light Blue
12. Grey
13. Brown
14. Dark Green

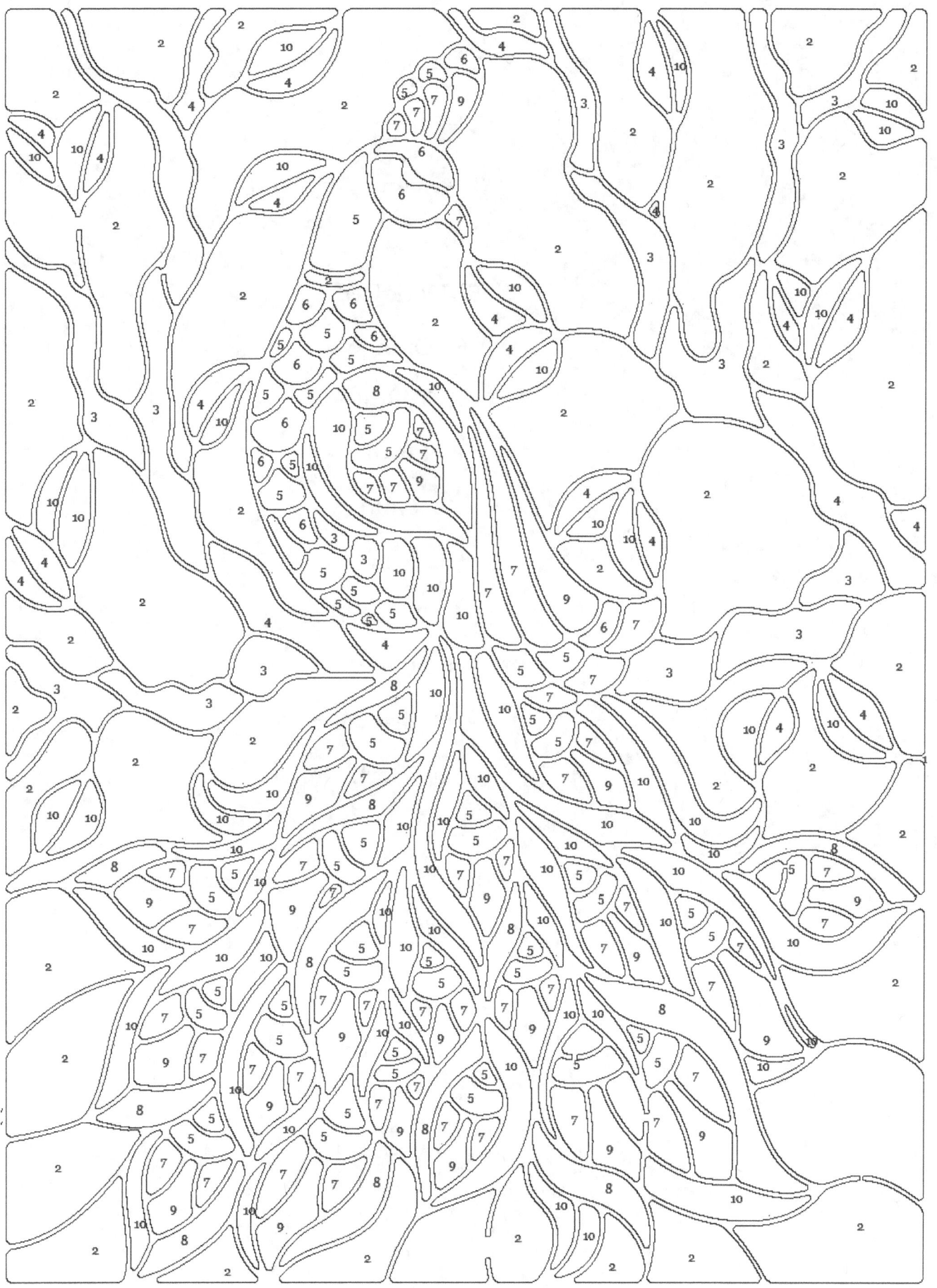

1. Black
2. Blue
3. Green
4. Red
5. Dark Red
6. Orange
7. Yellow
8. Purple
9. Gold
10. Pink
11. Light Blue
12. Grey
13. Brown
14. Dark Green

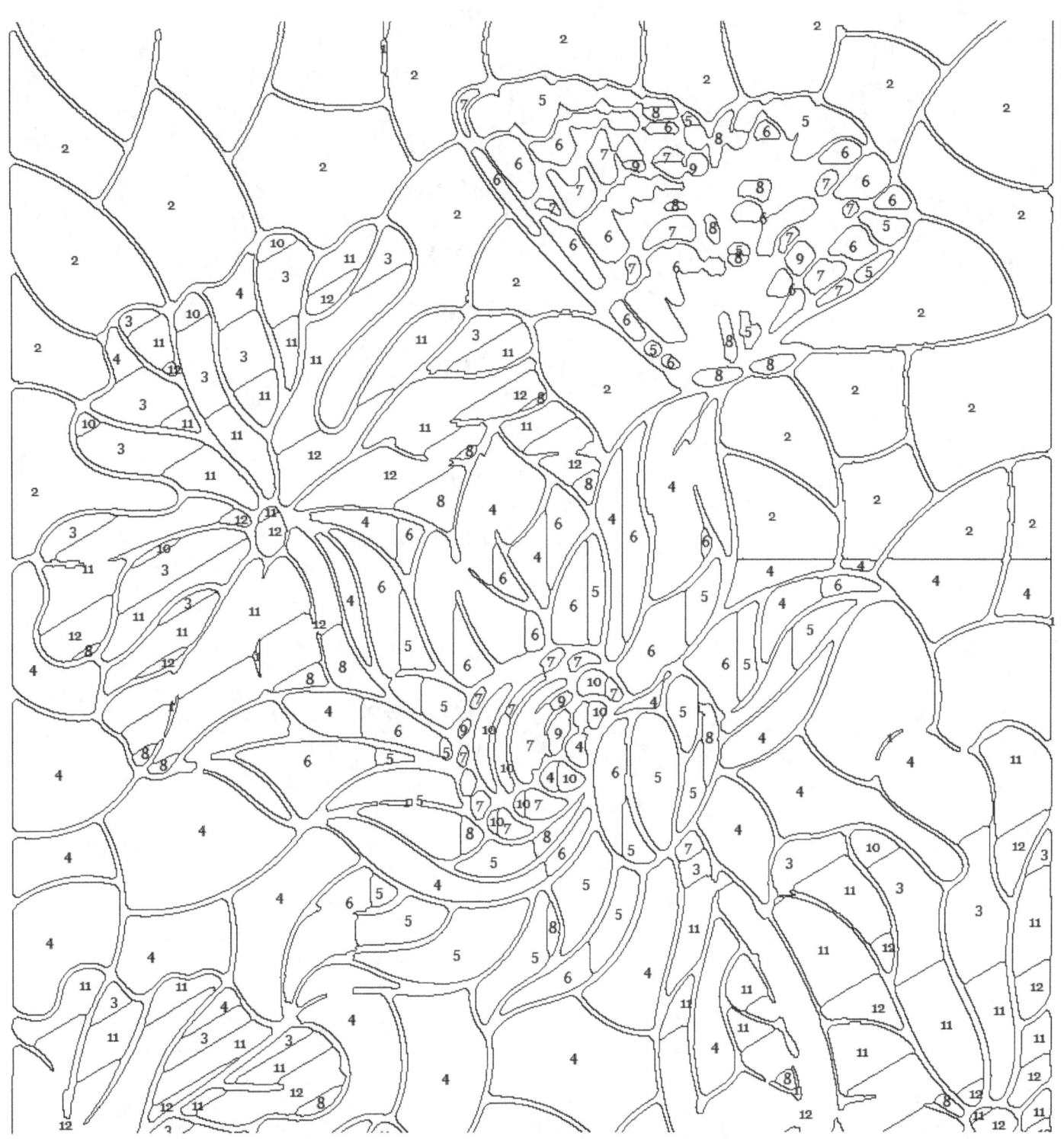

1. Black
2. Blue
3. Green
4. Red
5. Dark Red
6. Orange
7. Yellow
8. Purple
9. Gold
10. Pink
11. Light Blue
12. Grey
13. Brown
14. Dark Green

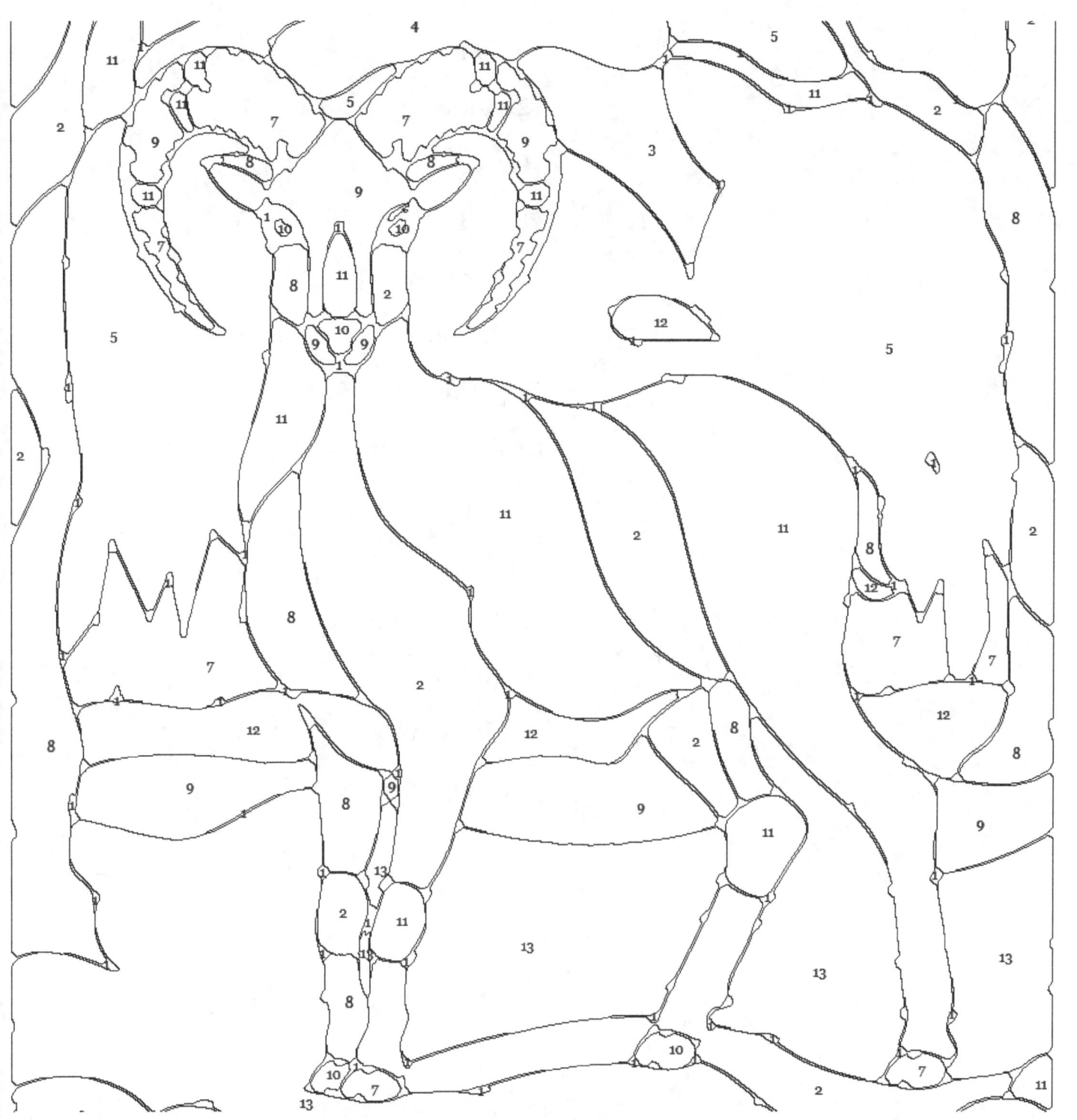

1. Black
2. Blue
3. Green
4. Red
5. Dark Red
6. Orange
7. Yellow
8. Purple
9. Gold
10. Pink
11. Light Blue
12. Grey
13. Brown
14. Dark Green

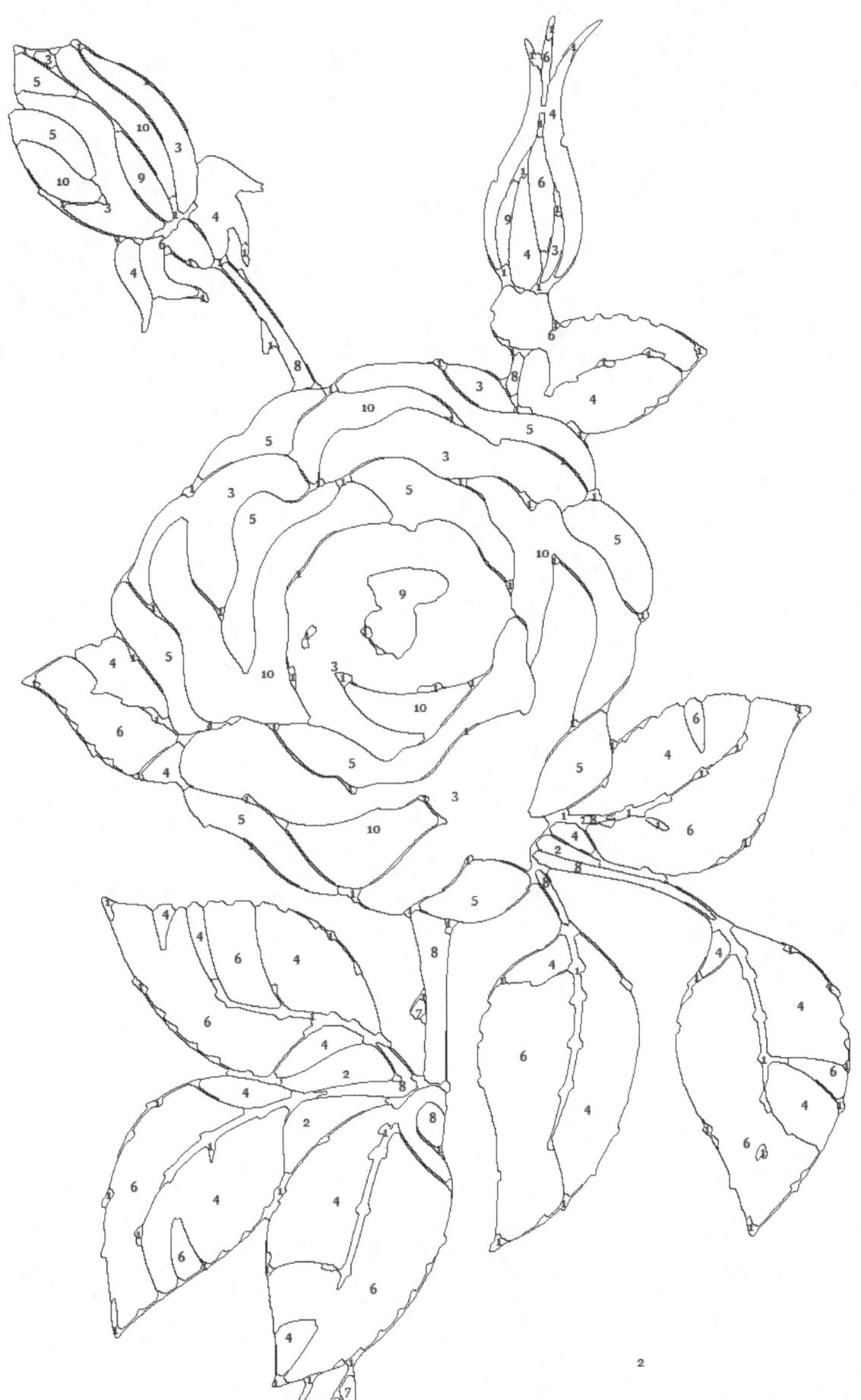